RUGBY

EXPLAINED

A GUIDE TO
UNDERSTANDING THE GAME

BLACKWATER PRESS

Peter McKenna

Editor
Claire Rourke

Design & Layout
Paula Byrne

Illustrations
Yahui Minnock

Cover Design
Karen Hoey

ISBN 978-1-84741-171-6

© 2007 Peter McKenna

Produced in Ireland by
Blackwater Press
c/o Folens Publishers
Hibernian Industrial Estate
Tallaght
Dublin 24

Contents

Introduction

Rugby union is the complete game. A sport for everyone – all shapes, sizes, intellectual abilities, social standing, ethnic background and (both) sexes. It is the definitive all-inclusive game. Whether a player is 7 foot tall or 5 foot small, 20 stone heavy or 9 stone light, there is a position in the team designed to meet that player's physical size. It is a team game where everyone is equal, contributing to the singular goal of winning. There may be star players on the team but, at the end of the day, a win is only achieved through the contribution of all players.

Rugby is a tough and confrontational sport where one team seeks to out-muscle the opposition for possession of the ball and then use its players' athletic ability to evade the defenders in order to score points. It is fast moving and physically hard. However, it is also a complex sport made up of simple concepts and copious rules and it requires intense mental application during play. Why did the scrum-half take a quick tap penalty near the halfway line rather than just let the ball be kicked to touch? Nothing happens at the elite level without a reason. There is a very simple and logical answer to the question posed above but it is an answer that involves knowledge of the laws of the game together with an appreciation about how these laws can be used to a team's advantage. This is the thinking side to the game of rugby and the purpose of this book.

Rugby Explained is all about understanding rugby. It is a learning manual for those new to the game and a refresher course for the experienced follower. It is a reference guide for player and supporter alike that takes a comprehensive look at the various aspects of this wonderful game and explains the basics as well as the intricacies of the sport in an easy to understand manner. The book explains why teams do what they do when they do it. It was written for those who are looking to deepen their enjoyment and knowledge of the game. I hope you learn something new and interesting about this fascinating game.

Peter McKenna
August 2007

Author's Note

Rugby union is a game followed and played by both genders with, it seems, equal enthusiasm and commitment. I have used the male gender throughout this book for convenience purposes only. The laws of the game apply to players regardless of gender and no slight or insult is intended.

The laws of the game that I have referred to in this book are for international level rugby union. There are slight variations to these laws which apply to the amateur game.

I have also included a glossary of rugby terms at the back of the book, many of which I have used throughout *Rugby Explained*.

About the Author

Peter McKenna is a former professional rugby player who represented Leinster and Ireland during a successful four-year career between 1999 and 2003. For the past two years, Peter has featured as a regular commentator for the Setanta sports channel. A qualified solicitor, he is a partner in McKenna Durcan, a Dublin-based law firm specialising in commercial and sports law.

Acknowledgements

Publication of this book has been made possible by the generous support of Bank of Ireland who are at the forefront of supporting rugby at all levels in Ireland. I would like to extend special thanks to Richie Boucher.

To John O'Connor of Blackwater Press and Claire Rourke for their great efforts in making the idea a reality. I also would like to acknowledge the kind support I have received from all at Setanta sports. The Brennanstown crew, thanks for the advice and encouragement. Someday, I will pay you back. You have been warned! Dave Keane for helping ensure the complicated laws can be understood and enjoyed and Fiona Kearns in Wishbone for her kind assistance.

To Mitchel Barry for the inspired words and guidance. Maresa Durcan, for her insightful suggestions and generosity of time and effort on my behalf. My family for their unconditional support and endless encouragement.

And, finally, to Gillian for her tremendous effort in all aspects of this book and for her incredible patience. Never before has so much been put up with by someone so lovely.

Peter McKenna
August 2007

A Word from our Sponsor

We're delighted at Bank of Ireland to be sponsors of 'Rugby Explained' and are confident that it will make a huge contribution to the understanding of the sport, and at the same time bring with it a greater appreciation and enjoyment of the game.

As sponsors of three of the Irish inter-provincial teams, we have witnessed unprecedented growth in this magnificent game in Ireland.

Today, our top rugby players are competing at the very highest level, both on the European and World stages, and they have done much to awaken interest, and pride, among all sports fans. This has particularly manifested itself in the huge upsurge in children taking up the game and in spectator participation through attendance at matches and watching games on television.

Rugby is a game which has some quite complex rules but which are guided by fundamental basic principles. This book outlines the basic principles with great clarity and explains the rules in the context of those principles. As such it demystifies the game for those who might not have played rugby and enhances the appreciation of strategy and tactics for current and former players.

Whether you're an active or a passive rugby fan, or simply want to discover more about the game, I'm confident that you'll find lots to interest and educate you within the following pages.

Richie Boucher
CEO Retail Financial Services Ireland
Bank of Ireland

1 BACKGROUND TO THE GAME

What is Rugby Union?

Rugby union is a fast-moving, physical, mentally demanding and competitive contact sport where two fifteen-man teams – made up of eight forwards and seven backs – contest for possession of an oval-shaped ball. Both teams compete to move the ball down the playing field towards their opponents' half by carrying, passing and kicking the ball to make as many points as possible by scoring tries (5 points), conversion kicks (2 points), penalty kicks (3 points) or drop goals (3 points), with the team scoring the greater number of points being crowned the winners.

History of the Game

Legend has it that the game of rugby union was conceived when, in 1823, William Webb Ellis, a pupil of the Rugby School in the English midlands, picked up the ball during a football match being played at the school and ran with it 'showing a fine disregard for the rules of football as played in his time', as the plaque in the grounds of the Rugby School proudly states. This version of events explaining the origins of the game is now accepted by sports historians as being far-fetched and a gross distortion of what is known to have happened.

What we do know for sure is that rugby union was commonly called rugby football back in Victorian times and it will come as no surprise to learn that it is a cousin of football. Handling the ball was permitted in football in the early 1800s and, indeed, right up until the formation of the Football Association in the 1860s. The Football Association even considered whether to allow its continuation, before eventually deciding to outlaw it.

Early rugby rules (known as 'laws') dictated that point scoring was limited to the kicking of conversions – no points were awarded for a try, only for successful conversions. All that a team that had scored a try was entitled to do was to attempt the conversion and thus have a 'try' for goal.

Below are some of the more interesting historical features of the game of rugby.

- A scrum could go on indefinitely, frequently for over twenty minutes at a time.

- A team at one time consisted of twenty-five players. It was reduced to twenty players in 1863 and further again to fifteen players in 1875.

- Up until 1871, it was possible to 'hack' and 'hack over'. Hacking involved kicking an opponent's shins and hacking-over meant tripping a player when he had the ball.

- Players would line up in scrums in the order in which they arrived as players did not specialise in a given position at the scrum.

- The dead-ball line was introduced following incidents like that which allegedly took place in a match at Newport in Wales where, on an exceptionally windy day, a player chased the ball over the goal-line for some 300 yards before he eventually caught up with it and touched it down to claim his try.

- The rules (laws) have changed considerably in the past hundred or so years and the modern game of rugby is a very different version of its former self.

Rugby League v. Rugby Union

In 1895, twenty-two clubs in northern England broke away from the Rugby Football Union (RFU), the country's governing body for the sport, to form the Northern Football Union. The reason for the split was that the RFU refused to allow the clubs to compensate their players for the time the players devoted to the game at the expense of their own livelihoods. The Northern Football Union was renamed the Rugby League in 1922.

Rugby union was committed to staying amateur, where players were volunteers and elected to play the sport not for pay but for the love of the game. This is how the sport of rugby union remained until 1995.

Rugby League clubs were professional from the time of the league's formation and paid their players like employees. In order to finance this professional game, the Rugby League recognised that they needed to make the game more attractive to watch in order to entice paying spectators on a consistent basis. Therefore, they designed changes to the laws of the game over time, the most dramatic of which that exist today are listed below.

- The number of players was reduced from fifteen to thirteen, which created more space on the pitch for players to attack and score tries.

- Teams must score within six tackles otherwise possession is handed over to the opposition – unlike rugby union where the team with the ball can suffer unlimited tackles and retain possession.

- Lineouts were abolished.

- A tackled player can hold on to the ball, get up on his feet and then release the ball by rolling it back between his legs to a team-mate. In rugby union, a tackled player must release the ball immediately.

As mentioned above, rugby union went professional in 1995 and all the top players are now paid by their clubs and/or union.

The Modern Game

Rugby union has changed dramatically since the days of Webb Ellis. Changes to the laws of rugby union have been brought in over the years to improve the safety of the game and to encourage more attacking play. For example, the points attributed to the various modes of scoring have changed from the days of a try being worth nothing, to 1 point, then 3 points, then 4 points until, today, when a try is worth 5 points (to discourage taking penalty kicks and instead encourage scoring tries). The game is constantly evolving and new changes to the laws of the game have been introduced in recent times by the International Rugby Board (IRB), the world governing body for the sport, in the realisation that the various unions and clubs need to generate greater revenue. It was recognised by the IRB that revenue in the game of rugby would be created through such means as gate receipts, broadcasting rights and sponsorship. In order to attract these forms of financial support, the game needed to be attractive to watch. Rugby needed money and there were many other sports vying for the public's attention. The game had to change – and it has.

The law changes that have been brought in over recent times ensure that the ball is kept in play for longer and that teams are rewarded for using the ball and scoring tries. The Super 14 and European Rugby Cup (aka the Heineken Cup) reward teams in the competitions for scoring four tries or more in a game by awarding them a bonus point.

The IRB carried out a statistical comparison and analysis of international games played in 1983 to those played in 2003, and made some very interesting findings. They noted that, in 2003:

◎ the ball was in play 40 per cent longer;

◎ there were three times more rucks/mauls per game;

◎ there were twice as many passes in a game;

◎ handling and kicking errors were halved and turnovers were four times less likely;

◎ there were almost 40 per cent fewer penalty kicks; and

◎ 50 per cent more tries were scored.

The laws of rugby union are still being amended and modified constantly in order to increase the safety of players but also to try to make the game more exciting. It has been a difficult formula for the IRB to get right. As the laws of rugby union have changed to increase the speed of the game and ensure the ball is alive in play for longer, the game has become more physical and contact more forceful. Players are stronger, bigger, fitter and more physical than ever. Pre-1995 and the game going professional, the average international back would have weighed 80 to 85 kilograms. Today, the average weight for an international back is somewhere between 95 to 100 kilograms. In fact, where once the winger would have been one of the lightest players on the team, they now regularly weigh over 100 kilograms. Players are not only getting heavier, they are also lessening their body fat. Before the professional era, the body fat for the average international back would have been around 12–17 per cent. Due to the conditioning work, dietary advice and monitoring players now receive, the body fat for a back is closer to 8–12 per cent. So while players are gaining more weight, a huge proportion of that increase is muscle. Players are able to tackle harder and at the same time withstand the increased physicality.

This advance in the conditioning of players has meant that international games are now played at an electric pace for the whole match by players in peak physical condition with little let up in the frantic tempo from start to finish, much to the delight of the rugby supporter.

Rugby Trivia

Below are some famous names who played rugby.

Che Guevera	The revolutionary played as a medical student whilst attending the University of Buenos Aires in Argentina.
Bill Clinton	The future US president played rugby during his time as a student with Oxford University.
George Bush Jnr	This US president played for the Yale 1st XV when he was a student at the Ivy League university.
Daniel Craig	The James Bond star played for Hoylake Rugby Club near Liverpool.
Anthony O'Reilly	The media mogul, former chairman of Heinz and one of Ireland's richest men played for Ireland and the British and Irish Lions.
Ernie Els	Famous as one of the top golfers in the world, Els was a decent rugby player and even better tennis player in his youth. He chose to concentrate on golf after he won the Junior World Golf Championship in the thirteen to fourteen-year-old category in 1984.

The USA are the reigning Olympic champions at rugby. They won the gold medal in 1924 – and rugby hasn't been an Olympic sport since.

There has only ever been one joint try awarded in international rugby when the referee was simply unable to decide who grounded the ball. It was scored by Howie Jones and Harry Peacock of Wales against Ireland in 1930.

French rugby player Gaston Vareilles missed his international debut against Scotland in 1910 – because of a sandwich. When the team train stopped at Lyon, Vareilles jumped off in search of food. However, the queue was so long at the buffet that, by the time he returned to the platform, the train was disappearing into the distance. He was never picked for his country again.

The whistle was only introduced into the game back in 1883. Before that, a referee had to shout his decisions.

The President of the IRFU, Frederick Browning, was shot dead during the 1916 Rising when his unit of the Veteran's Corps was returning to Beggar's Bush Barracks after a route march on Easter Monday.

2 BASICS OF RUGBY

General Laws of the Game

Before looking at the individual components that make up the game of rugby, below are some general laws of the game.

- Games are made up of two halves of forty minutes each plus time added for any injuries, with a half-time break of not more than ten minutes.

- Any player on the pitch may handle or kick the ball when he has it in his possession.

- A try is awarded when an attacking player grounds (i.e. places) the ball on or over the goal-line (better known as the tryline) of the defending team. A try is worth 5 points.

Ronan O'Gara reaching for a try for Ireland against Wales.
© Inpho

- After a try is scored, the scoring team is allowed a conversion attempt where the scoring team's kicker 'place kicks' the ball off the ground from anywhere near the 22-metre line (see the diagram of a pitch on page 10), but opposite the point where the try was scored. His intention is to kick the ball between the H-shaped goalposts and over the crossbar. If he is successful, his team is awarded a further 2 points.

- When a team is awarded a penalty within kicking distance of the other team's goalposts, it may elect to take a kick at goal. If the kicker is successful in kicking the ball over the crossbar and through the posts, his team receives 3 points.

- A drop goal happens in general play when a player strikes the ball on its upward bounce after it has been deliberately let drop to the ground and directs the kick towards the goalposts. If successful in kicking the ball over the crossbar and through the posts, his team receives 3 points.

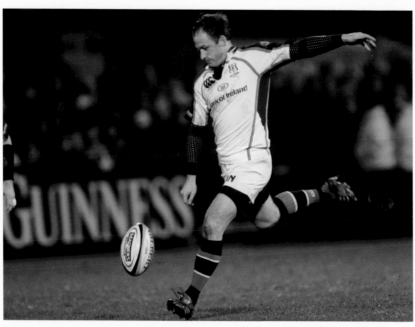

David Humphreys of Ulster and Ireland – a master of the drop-kick.
© *Sportsfile*

- After points are scored, the game is restarted by the ball being drop kicked back to the scoring team by the opposition from the middle of the halfway line.

- Passing, pushing or throwing the ball forward, even unintentionally, is not allowed. The ball may only be passed, pushed or dropped laterally across or backwards, although it may be kicked forward.

- A player may not have the ball kicked to him by a team-mate if he is in front of the kicker.

- Players in possession of the ball may be tackled anywhere from the shoulders down – above the shoulders is deemed a high tackle and, if it happens, a penalty is awarded against the tackler.

- Only the player with the ball may be tackled. A tackled player who falls to the ground must immediately pass or release the ball, and the tackler must immediately release and roll away from the tackled player.

- A scrum restarts play after a forward pass or when a player has dropped the ball forward after it has hit off his hands or arms (but not any other part of his body), which is known as a knock on. A scrum can also be awarded in the situations outlined on page 23.

- A lineout restarts play after the ball travels into touch, when the ball or the person carrying the ball touches the sideline ('touchline') or the ground beyond the touchline – otherwise known as out of play.

- The referee is responsible for making sure that everyone follows the laws of the game and plays safely. He will also keep a record of the time and the score. However, he is also advised by his touch judges of any 'off the ball' player indiscretions that he may not have seen. In those circumstances, the referee may ask the touch judge to recommend a course of action (i.e. warning a player, awarding a penalty, etc.) and the referee chooses whether or not to follow these recommendations.

- The touch judges' other jobs are to determine where the ball went into touch and to indicate if the ball was kicked through the posts and over the crossbar for penalty and conversion kicks. A touch judge can always be overruled by the referee.

- For international test matches, and in the major club competitions, there is an extra official called a TMO (television match official). The TMO is there in case the referee needs assistance in deciding whether or not to award a try and whether or not a penalty kick or drop goal was successful. The TMO makes a determination after reviewing the television footage immediately after the incident has occurred. The individual referee decides if and when to use the TMO.

The Playing Field

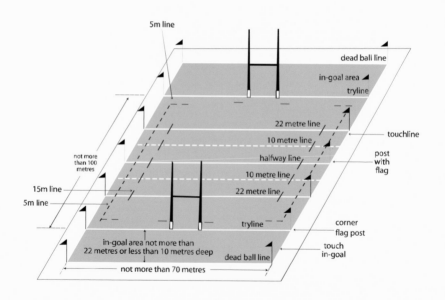

The rugby field, better known as the 'pitch', is a maximum of 100 metres long, from tryline to tryline, and 70 metres wide. At each end of the pitch, there is an in-goal area, which is no more than 22 metres long. The field is marked by a halfway line, two 10-metre lines, two 22-metre lines and two dotted hash lines on either side of the pitch, 5 metres and 15 metres respectively from the sideline and extending from tryline to tryline. There is a set of H-Shaped goalposts on each tryline.

Below are further explanations of the different areas of the pitch.

◎ **Dead-Ball Line:** One of two lines marking the lengthwise boundaries of the field, located at the back of the in-goal area, a maximum of 22 metres from the tryline. It marks the boundary line at the end of the pitch past which is out of play.

◎ **In-Goal Area:** The area between the tryline and the dead-ball line, and between the touch-in-goal lines. A try can be scored either on or over the tryline once it is within the in-goal area.

◎ **Tryline:** Also known as the goal-line, it extends across the pitch. The trylines are a maximum of 100 metres apart. Again, the opposition must ground the ball either on or over this line in order to score a try and receive 5 points.

◎ **22-Metre Line:** One of the solid lines running across the field, 22 metres from each tryline. The 22-metre line marks out the '22-metre zone' which is the area between the tryline and this line. The 22-metre line is also the line behind which 22-metre drop-outs are taken.

◎ **10-Metre Line:** One of the dashed lines running across the field, 10 metres from the halfway line. A kick-off from the halfway line must travel across this line in order for play to continue.

◎ **Halfway Line:** The line that extends all the way across the field at the midpoint of the pitch. It marks the division between the two teams' territories. Kick-offs are taken from the centre of this line.

The touchlines, touch-in-goal lines and dead-ball lines are not considered part of the playing area of the pitch and therefore if the ball or the ball carrier touches any of these lines, the ball is considered to be out of play. The corner flagposts are considered to be part of the touch-in-goal lines and, again, if the ball or the ball carrier touches the corner flagposts, the ball is considered to be out of play.

The Positions

THE TEAM

Each team has fifteen players and each player has a distinct position within the team. Individual players' positions are made clear by the number they wear and each position carries with it a particular role.

The following diagram illustrates the various positions with their respective numbers that appear on the back of the players' jerseys.

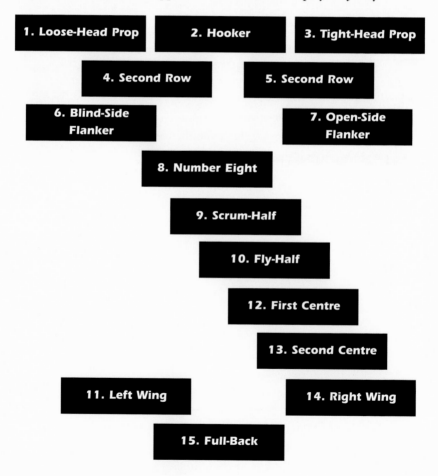

As already mentioned, each position involves a particular role and function within the team and these are explained further below.

No	Position	Role in the team
15	Full-Back	The last man in defence, primarily responsible for fielding opposition kicks. The full-back covers a huge amount of ground during a game and organises his team's defence from his position at the back of the field. He is also used as a potent attacking runner who can appear anywhere in the backline. Normally, he will enter the backline down the channel between the second centre and winger.
14	Right Winger	Usually one of the quickest players on the pitch. The right winger is most dangerous when he receives the ball in space out wide. With the other two members of the back three (the left winger and full-back), he is responsible for fielding opposition kicks.
13	Second Centre	One of the quicker backs, the second centre is normally big, strong and fast and can be used as one of the main attacking threats. He is also responsible for distributing the ball to the other outside players (the wingers and full-back) in space. In defence, he plays a key part in ensuring the opposition outside backs do not break through the defensive line.
12	First/Inside Centre	There are two types of first centres. Most northern hemisphere first centres are big and strong and are used primarily to run straight and hard and get over the gainline. In the southern hemisphere, a first centre is used like a second fly-half with the same kicking and distribution responsibilities. In defence, he is one of the strongest defenders and is often used to protect and assist his fly-half in tackling the opposition.
11	Left Winger	This position has the same role and characteristics as a right winger, except he stands out wide on the left. However, like the right winger, there is nothing preventing him from appearing as an extra man by 'coming off' his wing and joining an attack going from the left-hand side of the pitch to the right-hand side. Wingers are usually the top try scorers on a team.

No	Position	Role in the team
10	Fly-Half/Out-Half	Along with the scrum-half, the fly-half is one of the main decision-makers when it comes to determining how his team's possession of the ball is to be used. He must be cool under pressure and often the best footballer, skills-wise, on his team. He is generally responsible for kicking for points and the distribution of the ball.
9	Scrum-Half	The scrum-half is the link between the forwards and the backs. He handles the ball at the most critical times in a match and his decision-making ability must be excellent. He feeds the ball into the scrum and regathers it from scrums, lineouts, rucks and mauls, and is responsible for getting the ball away from the place of contact to his fly-half. In fact, nearly 50 per cent of all passes in a game are made by the scrum-half. Therefore, the scrum-half must have a fast, long and accurate pass. He is normally one of the smallest players on the pitch, but must be tough because he is generally the first of the backs in defence that will come in contact with a big, attacking forward.
8	Number 8	The central figure in the back row, the number 8 is often used as an attacking runner from the back of scrums. Like the other two members of the back row (the two flankers), he is responsible for getting to a loose ball and the breakdown first.
7	Open-Side Flanker/Wing-Forward	Takes his name because he is always positioned on the 'open-side' of the scrum, meaning the side furthest from the sideline. He has the same back-row responsibilities in open play as the other members of the back row (the blind-side flanker and number 8) but generally is expected to be the first to the breakdown. A key link man between the backs and forwards.
6	Blind-Side Flanker/Wing-Forward	Binds on to the scrum on the side nearest the touchline. Often used as a jumper at the back, or 'tail', of a lineout. Does a lot of hard work at the breakdown and at the fringes of play. His efforts do not stand out like the open-side's, but his role is just as important.

No	Position	Role in the team
5	Second Row	This player binds on the right-hand side of the second row at the scrum. As he is generally one of the tallest players on the team he is normally one of the main lineout jumpers (normally in the fourth position in the lineout). He is also responsible for generating power to his props in the scrum through his leg drive.
4	Second Row	This player performs the same roles as number 5, except he binds onto the left-hand side of the second row at the scrum. Generally jumps in the second position in the lineout.
3	Tight-Head Prop	The tight-head prop is positioned on the right side of the front row. He derives his name from the fact that he interlocks his head inside the opposition's loose-head when the two packs engage at a scrum (see page 24). Normally, he is the prop most responsible for upsetting the opposition front row during their scrum in an effort to hinder their ability to control the ball. Used as a 'lifter' in lineouts, his job is to get the 'jumpers' as high in the air as possible by lifting and supporting them during their jump. In the professional game, he is valued much more than the loose-head.
2	Hooker	The hooker is normally the player entrusted with the crucial role of throwing the ball into the lineout. During scrums, he is found in the middle of the front row. When his scrum-half feeds the ball into the middle of the scrum, the hooker is responsible for 'hooking', or guiding, the ball with his right foot to his number 8 at the back of the scrum (see page 28).
1	Loose-Head Prop	This position binds on to the left side of the front row, with his head interlocked on the outside of the opposition's tight-head prop when the two packs engage at the scrum. He is the anchor of the scrum and is responsible for keeping it straight. His job is to make sure the hooker can get a good view of the ball when it is put in by the scrum-half. He is also used as a lifter in the lineouts.

Units

In addition to each player's position receiving a name, there are also names commonly used to describe units within the team. This is the remarkable thing about rugby – despite each player having an individual role and duties, a player will also form part of at least one unit that will have another responsibility, and again the player will have his greater role as part of the team itself. For example, the full-back will have his own individual tasks as described above, but, along with the left winger and right winger, he forms a unit known as the back three. Generally, the back three are the players who stay somewhat deep and behind the rest of their team-mates in defence in order to cover an opposition kick or defensive line breakthrough. The full-back will also have his 'team' role in ensuring the team's plan in attack and defence, as determined by the coach, is enacted and followed.

The unit names are used for descriptive convenience and include the following.

Numbers	Name of Unit
11, 14, 15	The back three
11 and 14	The wingers
12 and 13	The centres
11, 13, 14, 15	The outside backs
9 and 10	The half-backs
9–15	The backs or the backline
1–8	The forwards or the pack
6–8	The back row or the loosies
4 and 5	The second row
1–5	The tight five
1 and 3	The props
1–3	The front row

The Replacements

For an international game, a team can nominate seven replacements, numbered 16 to 22, who can be substituted for another player at any time during the game. There are two types of substitutes in rugby union – temporary and permanent.

The temporary substitutes come on for any player who has suffered a blood injury and who is permitted a maximum of fifteen minutes to go off and be cleaned up and to stop any bleeding. If the injured player returns to the pitch within fifteen minutes, the temporary replacement must return to the bench and can come on again at a later time if required, as a temporary or permanent replacement. If the injured player has not returned to the field within fifteen minutes, the temporary replacement becomes permanent.

Permanent replacements are substitutes who come on as a direct replacement for another player on the pitch. The replaced player is not allowed to return to the pitch. However, there is an exception allowed and that is when a front-row player who has been taken off for tactical reasons is permitted to come back on for another front-row player who becomes injured. A player who is substituted due to injury can under no circumstances return to play again in a match.

If another front-row player becomes injured or temporarily suspended (i.e. sin binned), and there are no more substitute front-row forwards available to replace him, scrums will become uncontested which means the scrums will continue as normal except neither side can push for the ball and the team with the put-in retains possession. Uncontested scrums were introduced as safety precautions in circumstances where there are no other front-row players available.

The replacements numbers and their usual positions are given below. For safety reasons, there must always be a prop and a hooker in the replacements.

16	Sub Hooker	**20**	Sub Scrum-Half
17	Sub Prop	**21**	Sub Fly-Half/First Centre
18	Sub Second Row	**22**	Sub Utility Back (11, 13–15)
19	Sub Back Row		

The Role of the Forwards

The main role of the forwards is to gain and retain possession of the ball by dominating their opponents in the set pieces of the scrum and the lineout. The number-one aim in rugby is to get possession of the ball and this is what forwards are primarily responsible for. There is a saying in rugby that forwards win matches and the backs determine by how much. Unless the forwards provide a steady supply of possession, the backs can do very little in attack as they don't have the ball.

Generally, forwards are larger than the backs and are traditionally stronger, but slower and less agile. However, the modern game has seen a change in the athleticism of forwards and many are now just as fast and adept in open play as their team-mates in the backs.

The Role of the Backs

The primary role of the backs is to use the ball won by the forwards to score points, either by running or kicking the ball. The key attribute for most positions in the backline is pace, especially at international level. In the modern game, all backs are expected to have strong distribution (passing) and catching techniques together with competent kicking ability off both feet. The fly-half is normally the team's points kicker and would be expected to have a success rate of 70 per cent plus in his kicking. Again, the type of person who would traditionally play in the backs – small, agile, fast – has changed with the advent of professionalism and this has brought substantial increases in player size and strength.

Kick-Off

A coin toss determines which team kicks off and the direction in which each team will play. The defending forwards about to receive the kick-off will spread out behind the 10-metre line across from their opposite numbers, marking them man for man, in preparation to receive the kick.

The kicker, who can be any member of the team, will kick-off from the middle of the halfway line using a drop-kick, most often kicking the ball high and short to the opposing forwards (though he can also kick it long and deep or away from the forwards). All the kicker's team must be behind the ball before it is kicked. The kick must travel at least 10 metres and land within the field of play. If the ball does not reach the 10-metre line or the kick goes long and bounces over the tryline into the in-goal area and is either grounded by a defender without delay or simply rolls out over the dead-ball line, the defending team have the option of a scrum back in the centre of the pitch on the halfway line or having the kick retaken. If the kick-off goes straight into touch without bouncing first, the defending team can elect to: (a) have the kick retaken; (b) take a lineout at the halfway line; or (c) take a scrum back at the centre of the halfway line. Invariably, the defending team will take the scrum because there is a better chance of retaining possession and there are more attacking possibilities from this area of the pitch available to them.

The second half of a match is started in the same way as the first, except the teams switch ends of the pitch and the team that kicked off the match now receives the kick-off.

Kick-offs are highly pressurised situations for the kicker and require precision and accuracy. The ideal kick-off is a kick that allows the kicking team time to run up and challenge for the catch or, at the very least, leaves the catching team with very little time or angle from which to make an effective returning kick. Not only do the kickers spend hours practising for kick-offs but the teams themselves will also spend a great deal of time practising their positioning and skills in defending kick-offs to ensure they secure possession.

Scoring a Try

Once an attacking player enters the defending team's in-goal area, he must 'ground' the ball to be awarded the 5 points for the try. A player grounds the ball by holding the ball and touching the ground with it or pressing down on the ball on the ground with his hands, arms or the front of his body from waist to neck inclusive (known as 'downward pressure'). As already mentioned, the tryline forms part of the in-goal area. The goalposts and padding surrounding them are also part of the tryline. If an attacking player grounds the ball on or over the tryline or against the base of a goalpost or padding, a try is scored.

On the tryline is still a try – Felipe Contepomi scores a try for Leinster despite the close attention of three Bourgoin defenders.
© Sportsfile

When an attacking player with the ball is tackled short of the goal-line but the player's momentum carries him in a continuous movement along the ground into the opponents' in-goal area, and the player is first to ground the ball, a try is scored. Indeed, if a player is tackled near to the opponents' goal-line so that this player can immediately reach out and ground the ball on or over the goal-line, a try is scored. If this is not done immediately, and is a delayed movement, it may be considered to be playing the ball whilst on the ground and be penalised by the referee.

Should the referee have any doubt about which team grounded the ball first, play is restarted by a 5-metre scrum, in line with the place where the ball was grounded. The attacking team will have the put-in at the scrum.

However, if the attacking player loses control of the ball in the in-goal area and does not touch the ball down on the ground and a defender instead grounds the errant ball, play will be restarted with a 22-metre drop-out for the defending team. Often a player will cross the tryline near one of the touchlines and will look to run, in the in-goal area, towards the posts before touching down. This is done to provide a better angle for the person kicking for the conversion points because the conversion kick must be taken from a place in the field of play opposite the spot where the try was scored. Thus the kicker's job is typically made much easier when the try is scored between the posts.

The conversion kick is taken immediately after the try. The defending team must retreat to the in-goal area but can rush the kick once the kicker has addressed the ball and has started his approach to kick it. The kicker can either place kick or drop kick the conversion (though the vast majority of conversions are place kicked).

Some More Laws

Below are some of the more specific laws that make up the game of rugby.

- ◎ **A penalty try:** This may be awarded if a team in possession of the ball is denied an almost certain try because of foul play by the opposition.

- ◎ **Fair catch or Mark:** This is when a ball is caught directly from an opponent's kick (i.e. without bouncing on the ground first) behind the catching team's 22-metre line (including the in-goal area). The player catching the ball calls out 'mark' and is awarded a free kick if his cry of 'mark' is heard by the referee. The catcher can elect to take a scrum at the place of the mark instead of the free kick if he should so wish. A mark cannot be called on a ball that is caught from a kick-off or 22-metre drop-out. In general, a catcher cannot be tackled when he is in the air, although the opposition are permitted to challenge for the ball.

- ◎ **Taking the ball into your 22-metre zone:** When a player carries the ball into his 22-metre zone (the area between the tryline and 22-metre line) by running back behind his 22-metre line and then kicks it straight to touch without the ball bouncing, unlike the normal situation, the lineout is awarded to the opposition in line from where the ball was kicked and not where it crossed the touchline. If, however, the ball is passed back to the kicker standing behind the 22-metre line by a team-mate standing in front of the 22-metre line, the lineout will take place opposite where the ball went into touch.

- ◎ **Touching a corner flagpost:** If an attacking player crosses the tryline but touches the corner flagpost before he has grounded the ball, the try is not awarded and the defending team gets a 22-metre drop-out. The corner flagpost is positioned on the touchline and as such is deemed out of play. Interestingly, a player may touch the flag on the corner flagpost and the try will still be awarded but he cannot touch the corner flagpost itself.

- ◎ **Kick rolling over the dead-ball line:** If a team kicks the ball and it rolls over the opponents' dead-ball line untouched, the opposition may be awarded a scrum back up the pitch at the point where the kick was made.

- ◎ **Accidental offside:** If an attacking player with the ball runs into his own team-mate in front of him and opposition players are in close proximity, the team-mate is deemed to be accidentally offside and a scrum is awarded to the opposition.

- ◎ **Ball touching the referee:** If the ball touches the referee and he is deemed to have interfered with play, the referee must immediately award a scrum to the team that was in possession.

- ◎ **Quick lineouts:** Once the ball has crossed the touchline and has not touched another person (i.e. spectator or player) and the lineout has not begun to form, a player can quickly throw in the ball to a team-mate or himself, as long as the throw-in goes 5 metres. The lineout can be taken anywhere down the pitch between the point where the ball crossed the touchline and anywhere back to his own tryline. A quick lineout is taken in an effort to catch the opposition's defence off-guard or to ensure possession if their lineout is weak and being dominated by the opposition.

- ◎ **Challenging:** A player cannot charge or push an opponent when both players are running for the ball, except if the contact is shoulder to shoulder.

- ◎ **Crossing:** Blocking an opponent in order to stop him tackling one of your team-mates by moving in front of the team-mate in order to act as a shield is called 'crossing' and is punishable by a penalty if a referee deems that the crossing in any way interfered with a defender.

- ◎ **Obstruction:** Standing in a position which stops an opponent from playing the ball is also considered to be obstruction. For example, flankers cannot suddenly block the opposition's scrum-half as he tries to advance around the scrum.

3 THE SET PIECE

Introduction

Other than a kick-off or drop-out, the only other method of restarting play is a set piece – a term generally used to describe scrums and lineouts. These set pieces are practised time and time again in training and are vital if a team is to win. They are the platform upon which a team will look to secure possession in attack, and are a means of disrupting and affecting the quality of the opposition's possession of the ball when in defence. During the 2007 Six Nations Championship, 78 per cent of tries were scored within three phases from a set piece.

Let's look at the different types of set piece and when they occur.

Scrums

WHEN DO YOU HAVE A SCRUM?

A scrum generally takes place after one of the following stoppages has happened.

- ◎ The ball has been knocked on by a player and the defending team.
- ◎ The ball has not been thrown in straight at a lineout and the defending team opts for a scrum.
- ◎ A player has given a forward pass to his team-mate.
- ◎ The ball was taken over the tryline by the attacking team but not clearly grounded to the satisfaction of the referee (who therefore cannot award a try).
- ◎ The ball has been taken into contact by an attacking team and the referee deems that it will not become available for distribution by the scrum-half within a reasonable period of time.
- ◎ A player with the ball has accidentally run into a team-mate who is in close proximity to the opposition.

Very often, after one of the above incidents has occurred, the referee will let play continue to allow the other team to take *advantage* of the mistake in play. However, if no advantage occurs, the referee will whistle for a scrum to be set at a spot where the mistake in play took place. The non-offending team is awarded the ball and given the 'put-in' at the scrum. The referee will never play advantage if the safety of the players is in question.

FORMATION

The Ulster front row prepares to engage. © *Sportsfile*

For a scrum, both sets of forwards engage, or 'scrum-down', in the following formation.

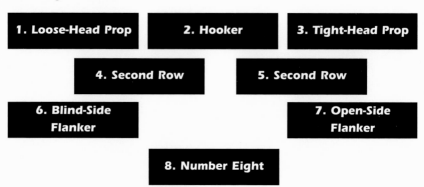

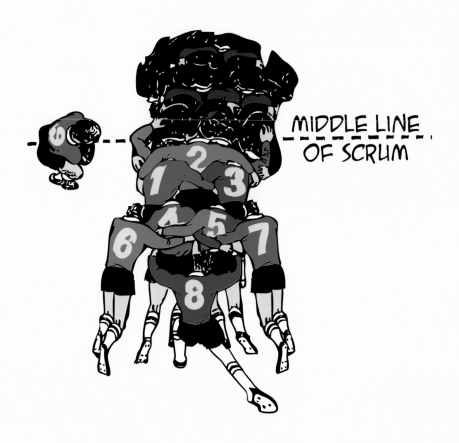

MIDDLE LINE
OF SCRUM

All eight forwards bind on to the player next to him (except the number 8) and push on the player(s) in front of him (including the number 8).

When everyone is in position, the referee will call the following sequence of play which must be followed by both packs.

1. **Crouch:** Both sets of forwards adopt a position where they have bound on to their own players and with bent knees and straight backs are ready to engage the opposition pack.

2. **Touch:** The loose-head and tight-head props touch their opposing prop on the shoulder.

3. **Pause:** Now that they are an arm distance apart, the referee gives both front rows a final chance to compose themselves before contact.

4. **Engage:** The two front rows, with their team-mates pushing from behind, collide together in a controlled fashion (known as the 'hit') and both sets of props adopt a bind on, and interlock heads with, their opposing props so that both packs are fully engaged and square-on with each other. They must also have their heads no lower than their hips. The back rows must remain bound until the scrum is over and this means binding with one full arm around a team-mate with a shoulder touching.

The scrum-half then feeds the ball into the middle of the scrum and the hookers strike for the ball with their feet.

The ball is then 'hooked' back by the successful hooker and 'channelled' back under the feet of his team's second row, towards the feet of his number 8, whereupon the ball is ready to either be used by the number 8 in an attacking move from the scrum or be distributed to the backs.

HOW ARE SCRUMS USED TO A TEAM'S ADVANTAGE?

There are several ways in which teams benefit from scrums.

◎ Scrums confine eight of the opposition players in one small area leaving the rest (90 per cent) of the width of the pitch available to attack into. A scrum opens up far more space out wide (i.e. on the other side of the pitch) to be exploited by fast backs.

◎ While scrums engage straight on, a dominant pack can drive and turn the scrum a few degrees to position the opposition's back row on the blind-side and effectively out of the defensive line – giving the dominant pack the ability to use their back row and all their backs to attack the wider spaced open-side of the pitch against an inferior number of opposition backs. It is illegal to intentionally wheel or whip-a-round a scrum. However, turning the scrum in the natural course of a drive or push is allowed.

◎ When a dominant pack engages and starts pushing the opposition backwards, the opposition are caught off-balance and it is harder to launch an attack or defence when the team is moving backwards.

◎ Psychologically, a team that is strong in the scrum and physically dominates their opponents undermines their opponents' self-confidence and saps their energy levels.

HOW DOES A WEAK SCRUM AFFECT A TEAM?

There are also several ways in which a weak scrum is damaging to a team.

◎ When the ball has been successfully hooked back but the opponents start pushing his team backwards, the attacking scrum-half will find it very difficult to pick the ball up and give a good pass to his fly-half. This, in turn, reduces the backline's ability to be successful in attack. As soon as the scrum-half feeds the ball into the scrum, a pack under pressure will look to channel the ball back to the feet of the number 8 and away from the scrum as quickly as possible before the opposition have a chance to push them off the ball.

◎ When the hooker wins the ball and his team starts pushing their opponents backwards, the team going backwards is caught off-balance and their defence is a second or two slower to rush up on the opposition. This gives the opposition backs time to compose themselves on the ball.

◎ When the opposition turns and wheels the scrum, the back-row defence is caught out of position and thus the defence is weakened.

◎ A team that is weak in the scrum must often change their style of play to avoid scrummaging against a superior pack. This will include electing to retake a lineout where there is a crooked throw-in rather than the usually taken option of a scrum. The downside of this is that lineouts provide less space out-wide to attack.

◎ Psychologically, a weaker team at the scrum loses confidence in its ability to physically dominate the opposition.

THINGS TO LOOK OUT FOR DURING A SCRUM

Below are some of the key areas to pay close attention to when there is a scrum.

- ◎ **The hit:** The engagement in the scrum, otherwise known as the hit on contact, that occurs when both packs interlock has as much psychological as physical importance. A big hit shows that a team is committed, determined and aggressive – not to be dominated. It is a statement of intent. A bigger hit also enables the stronger team to turn the opposition scrum to their advantage as described above.

- ◎ **Bind:** A pack that is tightly bound entering a scrum is far more effective in a scrum than a loosely bound pack. A successful scrum is not necessarily won by the biggest pack but where all eight forwards work together in unison.

- ◎ **The feed:** The feed is a term used to describe the scrum-half putting the ball into the scrum. The laws of the game dictate that the ball must be rolled into the middle of the scrum, however, despite a recent edict from the IRB stating that referees must be stricter in their application of this law, scrum-halves now tend to roll the ball in crooked to the feet of their second row. The crooked feed not only guarantees a team possession but it also lets the pack use a more powerful eight-man drive in the scrum instead of the usual seven-man drive, as the hooker no longer has to worry about hooking the ball thanks to the crooked feed. Without the need to hook, the hooker will not lift his feet off the ground which, in turn, stabilises the scrum. This helps the pack secure good ball because they are able to withstand the opposition eight-man shove. All this happens very quickly and the referee is looking out for so many possible infringements that they regularly miss the crooked feed.

- ◎ **Number 8 breaking bind:** The laws of the game say that the side that was not in possession of the ball when the scrum (and more particularly the front row) is wheeled 90 degrees, should have the put-in when the scrum is reset. When a scrum starts to be wheeled in this fashion, the number 8 will often break his bind early, pick up the ball and play on, to prevent the scrum being reset in the opposition's favour.

- ◎ **Offside:** At a scrum, the imaginary offside lines, which all other players not involved in the scrum must stay behind, are drawn across the field through the hindmost foot of the last person in each team's scrum.

INTERESTING FACTS ABOUT A SCRUM

- The IRB introduced the new four-phase sequence of actions before the scrum engages (previously it was just three phases: crouch–hold–engage) on 1 January 2007 to bring the front rows closer together and to take some of the risk out of the hit by slowing down and controlling the engagement.

- At the top level of the game, some two and a half tonnes of pressure flows through a prop's back during a scrum as a result of the pressure being exerted from behind by his team-mates and in front by the opposition pack.

- There are a possible seventy infringements that a referee must guard against during a scrum, including a crooked feed by the scrum-half, the tight-head prop binding incorrectly onto his opposing loose-head prop, and the defending back row breaking their bind before the scrum is over.

- Under the old laws of the game, there were fifteen players in each pack – now there are eight.

- The average number of scrums per game during the 2007 Six Nations Championship was seventeen. In 1983, in the old Five Nations Championship, it was thirty-one.

- In the 2007 Six Nations Championship, possession was retained by the team with the put-in 92 per cent of the time.

- In the 2003 Rugby World Cup, the team putting in the ball was awarded over four times as many penalties at the scrum as their opponents.

Lineouts

WHAT IS A LINEOUT?

If the ball goes into touch and out of play during the game, play is restarted with a lineout; this is similar to a throw-in in football.

The throw-in is normally taken by the hooker from the team that was not the last to touch the ball before it went out of play (into touch). An exception to this is if the ball is kicked into touch from a penalty kick. In that instance, the team that was awarded the penalty and kicked the ball to touch gets the throw-in.

The touch judge will indicate and mark the spot where the ball crossed the touchline by standing at the place with his flag raised above his head and the other arm pointing in the direction of the team who will throw in. If the ball bounces into touch, or is kicked straight into touch, from behind the attacking team's 22-metre line, the lineout is taken from where the ball crossed the touchline. If the ball is kicked straight into touch by an attacking team who were in front of their own 22-metre line, and the ball does not bounce before it leaves the field of play, the lineout is taken in line from where the ball was kicked.

FORMATION

To form a lineout, each team lines up in a row between the 5-metre and 15-metre lines (see illustration of these lines on page 32). The team with the throw-in determines how many players will be in each lineout – it can be as low as two (one jumper and one lifter) and as high as fourteen (all available forwards and the seven backs). The normal number of players in a lineout is seven and consists almost always of forwards.

The opposing team will line-up to match their counterparts and can have the same number, or fewer, players in the lineout – but not more – than the attacking team. Attacking teams vary the number of players they use in the lineout to keep the opposition guessing and make it harder for them to mark the jumper, thereby making it easier for the jumper to catch the ball. Attacking teams will shorten lineouts if they are experiencing difficulties from the opposition when throwing in to a full lineout or if they wish to use some forwards out in the backline for some special attacking move (i.e. have one of their big forwards run at, and hopefully through, a smaller defending back). A full lineout is preferred when the attacking backs want to confine as many of the opposition forwards in one area as possible in order to leave more space out wide to attack.

Andrew Farley taps the ball down to his waiting scrum-half –
Connacht v. Leinster. © Sportsfile

There must be a 1-metre gap between the two rows of opposing players
at a lineout. As already mentioned, the hooker is generally entrusted with
the task of throwing in the ball to one of his jumpers, traditionally a back
rower, who is supported high in the air by two team-mates called the
lifters.

The most common positioning of players during a lineout on the left side of the pitch is as follows.

				9						
	2	**1**	**4**	**3**	**5**	**6**	**8**	**7**		**Defending lineout**
2				**(1-metre gap)**						
		1	**4**	**3**	**5**	**6**	**8**	**7**		**Attacking lineout**
				9						

5m line   **15m line**

THE THROW-IN

Once the lineout has formed, a 'call' (a coded signal, so that the opposition won't understand) is shouted to the hooker and the rest of the attacking lineout by the forward in the lineout responsible for the decision. The call indicates where in the lineout the ball will be thrown and at what pace – for example, a slow lob throw or a fast throw to a player either jumping straight up, going backwards or rushing forwards. The hooker will then throw the ball (one handed or two handed) straight down the middle of the 1-metre gap separating the two lines, at a predetermined height for the intended receiver who, by this time, has jumped into the air. Most often, the throw is to the second rows who are jumping in the second and fourth positions in the lineout or to a back row player at the tail of the lineout. The lifters, positioned either side of the jumper, are allowed to boost the jumper higher into the air and to hold him there but they are not allowed to lift or support him below the knees. A crooked throw-in that does not go down the middle of the lineout will result in the opposition being given the option of the lineout being retaken with their throw-in or a scrum on the 15-metre line with their put-in.

Increasingly at the elite level, the hookers are actually throwing to a space and not a person. The call will tell the hooker where to throw the ball (at a spot 2–4 feet above the second position, fourth position or tail of the lineout) and the attacking jumpers will all starting moving around in the lineout, swapping positions, in order to confuse the defenders. The hooker throws the ball at the space (between 8-10 feet in the air) where he expects the jumper to be in the next few seconds. The jumper, assisted by the lifters, gets in position and jumps to the predetermined height and collects the ball. All this is done at speed and with great accuracy. When a lineout fails, it is not just because the hooker did not throw properly – it can also be as a result of the jumper mistiming his jump, a lifter not doing his job correctly, or a breakdown in communication and players getting the call mixed up.

THE CATCH

When jumping for the ball, a player must use either both hands or his inside arm to try to catch or deflect the ball. The jumper must not use the outside arm alone to try to catch or deflect the ball. If the jumper has both hands above his head, either hand may be used to play the ball.

Once the ball is caught, the jumper will do one of the following.

◎ **Drop the ball down from a height to the scrum-half:** This is called a 'tap down' or 'off the top' and is used to get the ball quickly to the fly-half via the scrum-half without the opposition back row putting undue pressure on him.

◎ **Land on the ground and then pass the ball to the scrum-half:** This is called a 'catch and give' and is used to make the opposition back row and backs hesitate and thus delay putting pressure on the fly-half.

◎ **Land and a driving maul (see page 44) will form on him:** This is called a 'catch and drive' and is used to suck in defenders who will try to stop the driving maul, which means that there is more space and fewer defenders out wide for the backs to attack when the ball is finally released by the scrum-half.

All the other players, from both teams, not involved in the lineout, except the scrum-halves, must stay 10 metres back from the lineout until it is over. The lineout is over when:

◎ the ball goes beyond the 15-metre line;

◎ the jumper taps down the ball to another player who carries it away from the lineout; or

◎ the hindmost foot of the last player in a maul that has formed has moved completely past where the lineout had originally formed or the maul moves beyond the 15-metre line. After the ball is caught, watch the referee's arm – it will be raised to remind the opposition backs to stay back 10 metres. Once the referee deems the lineout to be over, he will drop down his arm and the opposition backs can move forward up to the hindmost foot of the last player in the maul.

Players must not interfere with the opposition while the lineout is taking place. They are not allowed to tackle a player who is in the air, close the 1-metre gap or enter the 1-metre gap, unless it is in the act of jumping for the ball and not before the ball has left the hooker's hands. The ball must be thrown by the hooker a minimum of 5 metres before being played. The throw must be continuous and no feigning or 'dummy' throws are permitted. The ball may also be thrown completely over the heads of all players in the lineout and over the 15-metre limit so that a back can run up from his position 10 metres behind the lineout to catch it. However, this ploy is rarely used.

ATTACKING LINEOUTS

The forward responsible for making the call and deciding where in the lineout the ball will be thrown makes his decision based on a number of different criteria. Weather conditions play a role and the windier the day, the harder it is to make a straight throw over the various distances, therefore, shorter throws are favoured. At the higher levels of the game, videotape analysis of the opposition lineout will have identified their weaknesses and strengths. The attacking team's lineout will have its own strengths, which it will also look to exploit. Furthermore, the fly-half will also look at the team's field position and decide what type of ball he wants. He will look at where the space is and decide what lineout will deliver the type of ball he needs to launch a successful attack. He will then let the pack know where the ball should be thrown and how it should be delivered to him. Ideally, this is done in consultation with the forward responsible for making the lineout calls.

Below are examples of different types of lineout.

◎ **Ball caught at position number 2 in the lineout:** This is a safe ball and normally easy to secure. However, it also requires the scrum-half to make a longer pass to his fly-half and therefore the ball is in the air for a vital few extra seconds. To make matters worse for the attacking backs, the opposition back row will not have been engaged at the back of the lineout because everything is happening at the front of the lineout. Thus, thanks to the long pass from the scrum-half to the fly-half, the defending back row has an extra few seconds to join their backs in defence and so outnumber the attacking backs.

◎ **Ball caught at position number 4 in the lineout:** This a less safe option because it is a harder throw for the hooker to make accurately. The further the throw, the more room there is for error. Also, the opposition may look to put a jumper up at position number 3 or 4 in the lineout in order to get in front of the attacking jumper at position number 4 and disrupt the quality of ball the jumper is receiving. The benefit, though, for the attacking team is that the successful jumper has a number of options at his disposal, such as passing the ball straight to his scrum-half or to one of his forwards 'peeling' around the back of the lineout who will then run at the fly-half. The attacking team also knows that one of the opposition back row will most likely have been involved in lifting their jumper to contest for the ball and so the opposition back row are one player down. The attacking team also knows that the opposition back row, a man down, must also prepare for the peel around and will hesitate slightly before rushing at the fly-half just in case. All this adds up to give the attacking fly-half a few more seconds to compose himself on the ball.

◎ **Ball caught at position number 6 at the back of the lineout:** This is the most difficult throw for a hooker to make accurately. The long throw also gives the opposition extra time to react and contest for the ball effectively. However, it is also the best type of lineout possession for an attacking backline because the defending back row will be distracted and engaged at the lineout, leaving the seven attacking backs free to attack the seven defending backs.

DEFENSIVE LINEOUTS

The defending team will look to deny or at least disrupt the quality of possession for the attacking team, and will organise its lineout accordingly. The non-throwing side may or may not choose to jump and compete for the ball. If they do chose to compete and jump, they will usually watch the feet of the opposing players to get a sense of where the jumper is about to plant his feet in preparation for the jump. The defenders will then look to send up their own jumper in front of the opponent in order to catch the ball or at least hinder the opponent's ability to catch. When the attackers have a lineout close to the defenders' tryline, the defenders often elect not to jump to contest the catch but instead drive on to the opposing catcher as soon as he returns to the ground, and push the opposition pack backwards away from their tryline. Not contesting the jump in the lineout is a tactic often used by a smaller pack because the opposition will have a jumper and two lifters engaged in catching the ball and are, therefore, easier to disrupt and drive backwards by the defending team who have all their forwards set early in defence.

CONSEQUENCES OF A GOOD LINEOUT

One of the main benefits of a good clean catch is that the scrum-half receives the ball quickly and without too much attention from the opposition forwards. He can then distribute the ball quickly to the fly-half who receives the ball and has extra seconds to compose himself and launch the attack.

CONSEQUENCES OF A BAD LINEOUT

If the ball coming back to the scrum-half is of poor quality – i.e. the ball falls on the ground or the scrum-half receives the ball with an opposition forward bearing down on top of him – or if the ball is not cleanly caught by the jumper and it takes a few seconds to secure the ball and get it to the scrum-half, this gives the defence extra time to rush up, read the attack and match up the numbers opposite the attackers so that no gaps appear that can be exploited.

INTERESTING FACTS ABOUT THE LINEOUT

◎ Although hookers now throw the ball in at lineouts, previously it was generally the wingers' responsibility to do so. France experimented with their scrum-halves throwing the ball in at lineouts during the 1970s and 1980s.

- There were an average of thirty-one lineouts per Six Nations match in the 2007 championship. In the 1983 Five Nations, it was fifty-two. This shows that, today, the ball is in play much longer and therefore less restarts are required.

- In the 2007 Six Nations, possession was retained in lineouts by the side throwing in 85 per cent of the time.

- In over 1,500 lineouts in the 2003 World Cup, fifty-nine were called for not being straight.

The Unofficial Third Set Piece: The Kick-Off

Felipe Contepomi kicks off for Leinster.
© Inpho

The kick-off has now become as practised a method of restarting a game as the other set pieces. Kickers at the top level are exceptionally accurate thanks to the hours of practice they put into their craft. A kick-off is quite similar to a lineout in that a call is made prior to a kick-off, which is a coded signal given to the whole team, and lets each player know where the kick is going and what type of kick is going to be used. For example, the kick might go:

◎   short and to the left-hand side;

◎   long and to the right corner;

◎   short and up the middle of the pitch; or

◎   wherever the coach has identified as giving the best chance of challenging and reclaiming the ball.

The kick might go along the ground, be high and hanging, or long and direct. There are many variations that can be called, the intention behind each kick is to enable the kicking team maximum chance of reclaiming the ball by kicking to a weak section of the receiving team and making sure the kicking team arrive there in numbers.

4 THE BREAKDOWN

Introduction

The breakdown is a term used to describe the occasion during play, generally after a player has been tackled or held, when the ball is contested for by both teams. The breakdown is a highly competitive and physically combative area of play where the fittest, strongest, most courageous and skilful players battle for possession of the ball, sometimes over 150 times a game. Breakdowns can be very simple and straight forward – as when a tackle is made and the ball is immediately picked up off the ground by a team-mate and passed to a supporting player – or they can be complex and involve eight or nine players challenging for the ball. Typical examples of the breakdown include the following.

Tackle Area

Once he is tackled, a player must release the ball or he will be penalised. The area in which a player is tackled becomes what is known simply as the 'tackle area'. The tackled player is prohibited from playing the ball until he is back up on both feet. Likewise, the tackler must roll away from the tackled player and not do another act of play until he is also back on both feet. In the modern game, players who make the tackle are very good at getting back to their feet quickly and reaching over the tackled player on the ground and getting their hands on the ball before a team-mate of the tackled player gets to him in support. When a tackler wins the ball like this, it is called a 'turnover' – i.e. the ball has been turned over from the possession of the tackled player's team to his opponents.

OFFSIDE AT THE TACKLE AREA

The tackle area or zone is deemed to extend from the back foot of the tackler to the head of the tackled player. The angle at which the players involved in the tackle fall determines the size of the entry zone for the supporting players on either side. This entry zone is known as the 'gate'. All other players from both sides must enter the tackle area coming from the direction of their own goal-line and through the gate or they will be offside. Picture a sheep pen with a gate at either end of it and the tackled player and tackler are lying in the middle of the pen. This is the tackle area. The tackled player's team-mates can only enter the tackle area through the gate nearest their tryline. The tackler's team-mates can only enter the tackle area through the gate nearest their tryline. Neither players' team-mates can enter the tackle area from the side. However, a tackler getting back on his feet can come in from any direction once a ruck has not been formed.

Rucks

Clearing the ball from the ruck. © Sportsfile

A ruck occurs after a player carrying the ball is tackled to the ground by an opponent. As players from both teams rush in to try and secure the ball for their side, they come into contact with each other in a scrum-like formation, and thus a ruck is formed. The minimum number of players needed to form a ruck is two – one player from each team who are both on their feet. Once a referee has called 'ruck', no player is allowed to handle the ball. Both sides must look to drive their opponents off the ball and shoe the ball backwards using their feet, eventually making it available for their scum-half to pass. Should the ball not become available for distribution by either side within a reasonable period of time, the referee will award a scrum to the team moving forward.

Any player joining a ruck must stay on his feet. Falling down over the top of a tackled player is called 'going over', or 'diving over', and is not allowed. Players must join a ruck from behind the hindmost foot of the hindmost player and bind on to a team-mate, otherwise they will be offside and penalised.

When a player goes into contact with an opponent and falls to the ground with the ball, his primary job is to make sure the ball comes back on his side. Therefore, the player must ensure that he falls correctly (body parallel to, and facing back towards, his own tryline). He must then 'present' the ball back for his scrum-half by placing the ball on the ground towards his own team-mates, away from his body and any opposition defender – using his body to shield the ball from the opposition. The tackled player's team-mates will then look to drive any opponents off and away from the ball as described above, leaving it available for quick distribution to the backs to attack out wide, or for another supporting forward to simply pick up the ball from the back of the ruck, drive forward and create another ruck. This latter movement is called a 'pick and go'. A pick and go can be repeated again and again and is a useful method of keeping the ball moving forward and dragging defenders into the tackle area and, therefore, creating more space out wide for the backs to attack.

The scrum-half is the player best placed to judge how the ball should be used from a ruck. He will listen out for an urgent call from his fly-half demanding the ball but, in the absence of this call, he will direct the forwards to pick and go, or he might use a short pass to a forward runner to run at defenders around the fringe of the ruck in an effort to keep the ball moving forward and to suck in more defenders. The scrum-half may decide to run with the ball himself or to kick it into space for his winger to chase.

Mauls

Paul O'Connell organises the Munster maul.
© Sportsfile

A maul involves players on their feet holding the ball off the ground. A maul is formed when the player carrying the ball is held up by an opposition player but not put to ground. A team-mate then binds on to the held-up player and a maul is formed. The ball carrier will normally take the ball into a maul by intentionally turning his back to the opposition player. His team-mate will then securely rip the ball from him and stay bound, face-on, to him (with the ball carrier's back still to the tackler), so keeping the ball that bit further from opposition hands. More team-mates then join the maul in a controlled and predetermined formation – much like a scrum. The role of the supporting players is to form a wedge around the ball carrier ensuring the ball is shielded from the opposition.

Players must join a maul from behind the hindmost foot or they will be offside. A player must bind on to a maul using his whole arm, placing a hand on the maul is not sufficient and will be penalised. The ball is worked back from the initial ball carrier in the middle of the maul to the last player in the maul at the rear. When the ball is at the back, the last player must be fully bound on to the maul with at least one full arm.

DRIVING MAULS

This happens when a maul has been purposefully formed with the aim of using it to progress forward as a cohesive, attacking weapon. The forwards start to pump their legs, pushing against the opposition, moving the maul forward. The idea behind the driving maul is for the attacking team to keep possession of the ball, move forward and suck in defenders who must try to stop it. Thus, with fewer defenders out wide, extra space is created for the backs to attack. The scrum-half marshals the forwards and is responsible for directing them as he is the player with the best view of how the maul is progressing (all the forwards will have their heads down driving the maul) and determining the best time to release the ball to the backs.

If the ball carrier at the rear of the maul breaks off his hold of the other players in front of him, the maul has ended. If he then uses team-mates in front of him to act as a battering ram to drive forward, it is obstruction and this illegal move is known as 'truck and trailer', punishable by the awarding of a penalty to the opposition.

ROLLING MAULS

A rolling maul occurs when the attacking forwards form a maul and then roll it by moving the ball to the side of the maul where the defence seem weakest, detaching and quickly reforming the maul again with the attacking team tightly bound driving the maul forward. This can be an effective way of varying the point of attack and using the forwards' strength to gain field position.

A maul that is going forward and has momentum is very difficult to defend against. It is illegal to collapse a maul intentionally, so the defence must commit players to halting its momentum. The real trick is for the attacking team to release the ball as the maul is going forward and before it has stopped. The defence will be on the back foot and somewhat disorganised. This creates gaps for the attack.

If the referee deems that the ball has become unplayable or the person holding the ball has at least one knee on the ground, the referee will order a scrum to the opposing team. This is called the 'use it or lose it' rule. When a maul has stopped moving forward and become stationary, the referee allows five seconds for the maul to recommence its onward motion before he will deem the maul to be over. If the maul does restart within the five seconds, the next time the maul becomes stationary, there will be no further five-second window for it to restart. The maul will be deemed over and the team entering the maul with possession must immediately use the ball or lose it, at which point a scrum will be awarded to the opposition.

OFFSIDE AT A RUCK OR MAUL

Once a ruck or maul is formed, an imaginary offside line becomes present at the hindmost back foot of each team's side of the ruck or maul which extends from touchline to touchline. As more players join the ruck or maul, the offside line repositions to the hindmost foot of the last player to join the ruck or maul. All other players not involved at the breakdown must stay behind these offside lines until the ruck or maul is over otherwise they will be penalised. Below is a simple representation of this concept.

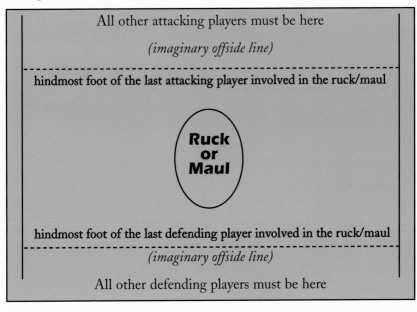

All other attacking players must be here

(imaginary offside line)

- -

hindmost foot of the last attacking player involved in the ruck/maul

Ruck or Maul

hindmost foot of the last defending player involved in the ruck/maul

- -

(imaginary offside line)

All other defending players must be here

5 ATTACK

The Three Ps

A successful attack involves the three Ps: possession, pressure and points. A team cannot attack unless it has the ball: possession. Retaining the ball and remorselessly going forward looking to attack the space puts the defence under tremendous strain: pressure. Relentless pressure will eventually cause the defence to break enabling the attacking team to score a try or be awarded a penalty kick: points.

The laws of the game are geared towards the attacking team. Scrums, lineouts and, to a lesser extent, the breakdown, are designed to enable possession to be retained by the side with the put-in, throw-in or which is entering contact with the ball. For example, a maul cannot be collapsed and once a ruck is deemed to have been formed, defenders can only use their feet to win the ball. Analysis by the IRB has shown that the team entering the breakdown with the ball at international level will retain possession in 95 per cent of cases. Defending teams at the set piece and breakdown will look to put pressure on the opposition and, hopefully, turn over the ball to their side, but in the vast majority of times, the ball will be retained. Attacking teams look to hold on to the ball, phase after phase, building the pressure and hoping to turn the possession into points.

Defending teams enter the set pieces and breakdowns more in the hope of turning over the ball rather than in expectation of it, and so plan and organise their defence in anticipation of the other team retaining the ball. The defending team must look to contain the attacking team and restrict their ability to receive the ball in open space by coming up in a line and tackling with gusto in the hope of forcing the attackers to make an error, concede a penalty or kick away possession.

The fact that the defending team hopes rather than expects to turn over possession during play means that they organise themselves accordingly and makes the attacking team's task of scoring a try that bit more difficult. To counter the organised defence, the attacking team must employ moves that will create space in the defensive wall for them to attack into. Deception is key and all the moves are designed to fool the defence. These attacking moves are carried out at pace and involve agility coupled with deft ball-handling skills. The attacking team must have the timing, understanding and courage to enact these moves in the face of an oncoming organised defensive wall. Such attacking moves are designed to exploit any weaknesses or chinks in the defensive team's armour.

Practising moves at an Ireland squad training session.
© Sportsfile

Attacking Rules of Thumb

Attacking moves are based on certain attacking maxims.

- ◎ The inside arm (arm nearest the scrum/lineout/breakdown) of a defender is his weakest defending arm.

- ◎ An attacker running onto the ball at an angle is harder for a defender to prepare to tackle than an attacker running straight.

- A player running at speed is harder to tackle than a player running at half pace.

- One-on-one, the quicker attacker will almost always beat the slower defender.

- An overlap created by unexpectedly bringing in an additional attacker will put added strain on any defence.

- Decoy runners pretending they are about to receive the ball will distract defenders and create space for an attacker to exploit.

- A player may be able to run faster with the ball in one hand but he can execute far more attacking options by carrying the ball in both hands.

- An isolated defender is a weakened defender.

- Turnovers are great attacking opportunities because the opposition defence will not be organised.

Common Moves Used

Attacking moves vary from the elaborate to the simple and take hours of practice to get just right. They can involve all seven attacking backs running at different angles and appearing in unexpected positions. Some of the more common moves include the following elements.

- **Miss pass:** This is where a player uses a wide pass to skip the player beside him to send the ball to the next player out wide. The hope here is that the defence will be slow to get out wide to defend and the attackers will make full use of the extra space. By moving the ball out wide quickly, attackers hope to get the ball to an attacker in space, isolate defenders and give their talented runners maximum chance to beat their individual opponent.

- **Dummy pass:** A dummy is a fake pass by a player to a team-mate. The player keeps the ball in both hands, looks at a team-mate as if he intends to pass to him, feigns making a normal pass but holds on to the ball. Hopefully the defender has 'bought the dummy' and drifted off the attacker onto the player he wrongly believes is about to receive the ball, leaving space behind for the attacker to utilise.

- **Switch:** This is where the ball carrier runs across the pitch hoping to attract and drag the defence with him. He then passes to a team-mate running back in the opposite direction, scissors-like, in the hope that the defender's momentum will make it difficult for him to stop and check the attacker.

- **Hidden runner:** This usually involves the full-back or wingers appearing unexpectedly inside or outside the ball carrier. The aim here is to momentarily confuse the organised defence by causing the defenders to commit to the attackers in front of them and leave space for the unannounced runner who has appeared out of nowhere to exploit.

- **Decoy runner:** This involves a player running at a particular angle and 'line' pretending he is about to receive the ball and hoping to distract defenders away from the intended receiver. This player must be careful because the laws state that if a player goes in front of a team-mate who is carrying the ball and interferes in any way with the opposition's defence, he will be penalised for 'crossing'.

- **Side-step:** A side-step is where a runner feigns going one direction (e.g. left) and instead plants his foot and accelerates in a different direction (e.g. right).

Most attacking moves employ at least one of these six elements. At its most simple, attack is geared towards creating a situation where the attack has the advantage in numbers (two attackers v. one defender, etc.), a mismatch (speed: fast v. slow; power: forwards v. backs) and momentum (going forward with the defence on the back foot).

In order for a move to be successful, all players in the attacking move, except the intended recipient, must look like they are about to receive the ball to draw the defence away from the intended 'strike zone'. The attackers must look to overload the communication lines between the defenders and cause utter confusion by creating so much movement and noise in front of the defenders that the defenders will all be distracted and shouting at each other at the same time looking for help and no one will hear what the other is saying. To achieve this, the other attacking players might call out to the ball carrier to pass to them, or they might run a decoy line pretending they are about to receive the ball, or do whatever they can to distract and deceive the defenders.

All these moves are carried out by the attacking team at a very fast pace in front of a defensive line that is coming up quickly in the hope of limiting the defence's reaction time.

An important point to note is that at a set piece outside the opposition's 22-metre zone, an attacking backline does not face seven defending backs. It actually is only attacking five backs. This is because the defending full-back must lie deep in anticipation of a kick. Furthermore, the defending blind-side winger must wait over on his side of the pitch in case the attacking scrum-half, supported by other attackers, runs down the blind-side, thus leaving five defending backs initially against a full attacking backline on the open-side of the pitch. This is why coaches design moves to bring the attacking blind-side winger and full-back into a move on the open-side in order to create an overlap and attack the space.

Brian O'Driscoll is able to off-load in the tackle to his
supporting team-mates.
© Sportsfile

Should any of these moves succeed and an attacking player breaks through the defensive line, it is vital that the ball carrier is supported by his team-mates otherwise the attack will break down should he encounter any more defenders on the way to the tryline. The support runners must work hard to get close to the ball carrier in order to be in position to receive a pass and continue the attack. The support runners should be coming from deep, at pace and varying angles in order to put the defence under enormous strain. Likewise, the ball carrier must be conscious of where the support runners are and work hard to link-up with them so that he does not become isolated and the defenders overwhelm him. The vast majority of tries are the result of very good support play.

Tactical Kicking

Kicking is the simplest way to get the ball over the gainline. It's also the easiest and safest thing to do when things go wrong and the team with the ball is being put under pressure by the opposition. A clearing kick to touch or down field will relieve the pressure and give the kicking team time to regroup and reorganise themselves.

Most tactical kicks are executed by the fly-half in an effort to advance the ball upfield and progress towards the opposition tryline. This is called 'territorial kicking' and is used as a tactic to establish an attacking team in the opponents' half which is the safest place from which to play.

When the ball is kicked with the intention of keeping the ball in the field of play, the kicker expects that one of his own fast-charging backs will recover the kicked ball before the opposition, or that one of his team-mates will tackle the opposition just as the opposition receives the kick. A team-mate in front of the kicker is offside until put onside by the kicker or someone who was behind the kicker overtaking that player when chasing the kick.

The trouble with kicking is that it is often very badly done – it requires judgement, decision-making, skill and organised team effort. Poorly executed kicks simply hand possession to the opposition. The thing to remember about kicking is that it is not just an individual act but a form of attack for the whole team. The kicking team must use what's known as an 'organised chase' in following up the kick. This involves the kicking team chasing the kick in an orderly fashion where they come up in a line and leave no space for the opposition to counter attack.

Other tactical kicks include an up-and-under (otherwise known as a Garryowen – named after the Limerick club that this type of kick was synonymous with), a chip kick and a grubber kick. An up-and-under is a kick where the ball is kicked very high but not very far. The idea is to put the receiving opposition players under incredible pressure by giving the kicking team time to get underneath the descending ball and challenge for it. A chip kick is highly effective and is used when a runner is faced with an on-rushing defender. The runner simply kicks the ball just over the defender and runs on to collect the ball. The defender cannot tackle the runner without the ball and is not allowed to intentionally impede the attacker's run to collect the kick. A grubber is a kick along the ground. This is most effective when the defenders are nearly on top of the attackers and a kicked ball is under serious risk of being charged/blocked down by the defenders. The kicker will simply toe the ball along the ground through a gap between the defenders (or their legs!) for his own players to rush on to in the hope of recovering the kick behind the defensive line.

Again, the most crucial thing when kicking the ball is not to gift possession of the ball to the opposition in open space, and so giving them plenty of time and room to counter attack. The kicking team's defence will be disorganised and vulnerable immediately after the kick. A loose kick that is unchallenged will give the opposition an opportunity to exploit any holes in the kicking team's defence as they are organising themselves. A precise kick that enables the kicking team to challenge for the catch, or leaves the opposition with very little space or angle to counter attack, is far more potent.

6 DEFENCE

Introduction

Statistical evidence compiled by the IRB shows that defence wins games. A team with an absolutely sound defence and an accurate goal kicker is far more effective than an exciting attacking team with a leaking defence. It's less attractive to watch but far more successful! Indeed, the common factor linking all the top international and club sides is that they all have a very organised, aggressive, water-tight defence.

There are two elements to a defence: the tackle and the defensive system.

The Tackle

Effective tackling is all about impact where the primary purpose of the tackle is to dispossess the ball carrier. The secondary aim is to stop the attacking team's momentum and prevent them from recycling the ball with ease.

The tackle technique of a top player will have been perfected over thousands of hours of training and playing the game from a young age right through his adult career. Without proper technique, the defender risks incurring serious injury, but poor technique will also result in the tackle not being effective and the attacking team may exploit this to their advantage.

There are four key ingredients to an effective tackle.

◎ **Position:** Back straight, body leaning towards the attacker and nearest shoulder aimed at the point of contact (thigh, chest, waist, etc.).

◎ **Hit:** The tackler's shoulder impacts against the chosen point of contact with all his weight in order to knock the attacker off-balance.

- **Wrap:** The tackler's arms wrap around the legs of the attacker in an 'iron-clad' fashion preventing the attacker from using his legs to stabilise himself, as momentum carries the attacker forward.

- **Drive:** The tackler uses the power of his legs to drive the attacker further off-balance and to the ground.

TYPES OF TACKLE

There are several different types of tackle that a player can make, depending on the situation he is presented with.

- **Front-on leg tackle:** This is the most common type of tackle. The defender faces the attacker, crouches and aims his shoulder at the area between the attacker's knee and hips, places his head to the side of the attacker and drives through using his leg power, whilst wrapping his arms around the attacker's legs. Of course, the hit can be anywhere below the shoulders, but the safest and most used tackle hit is on the thigh area.

Gavin Duffy of Connacht is tackled front on by
Bernhard Jackman of Leinster.
© Sportsfile

- **Rear tackle:** Normally employed after the ball carrier has breached the first line of defence and defenders are chasing the attacker from behind. The tackler, with his head to the side of the attacker's legs, hits with his shoulder, drives through with his legs to knock the attacker off-balance and wraps his arms around the attacker to haul the ball carrier to the ground.

- **Side-on tackle:** Normally employed when a defender is running across the pitch to tackle, e.g. open-side flanker (number 7) on the opposition fly-half (number 10). The same tackle basics – shoulder hit, head to the side of the attacker's legs, arm wrap, leg drive – are employed but, in this instance, are performed on the side of the attacking player.

- **Smother tackle:** Where the tackler aims to hit the attacker higher up on his body, usually around the chest but always below the shoulder. There is more emphasis on wrapping the tackled player up and so preventing him off loading the ball to a supporting team-mate. This type of tackle slows down the attack.

Brian O'Driscoll prevents Gavin Henson of Wales off-loading the ball in the tackle. © Sportsfile

- **Double tackle:** This is where one defender tackles the ball carrier low around the legs using a front-on leg, side-on or rear tackle, and at the same time another defender tackles the ball carrier high (always below the shoulder) looking to wrap up the ball so that the ball carrier is unable to release it and so the attack is slowed down.

Shane Horgan and Keith Gleeson, both of Leinster, join up to stop Ian Dowling of Munster in his tracks.
© *Sportsfile*

- **Dump tackle:** This is a very aggressive tackle where the defender makes a front-on tackle but instead of trying to haul the ball carrier to the ground immediately, he will look to hit and then pick up the attacker and drive him backwards eventually 'dumping' him to ground by falling with the attacker with his arms still wrapped around the player. A 'spear' tackle is very similar to a dump tackle but involves the defender hitting, picking up and driving the attacker backwards head first into the ground. A spear tackle is very dangerous and is, thankfully, illegal.

◎ **Ankle tap:** Unofficially this is another type of tackle. It does not involve any of the four basic ingredients of a tackle as described above (position, hit, wrap and drive) but, paradoxically, it is still effective. The tackler who is struggling to get close to the ball carrier makes a despairing lunge at him and strikes the nearest ankle of the ball carrier against the other ankle causing him to trip. The ball carrier is not considered tackled when he falls to the ground because he is not being held by a tackler. However, his attack has been momentarily stalled and the defenders are given an opportunity to catch and dispossess the attacker.

You might ask why every tackle is not a dump tackle or double tackle since they would seem to be so effective? The reason is because they are very difficult to perform and require the right conditions to be in place for a defender (i.e. an attacker running at a slow enough pace, straight and the defender who is set and in position ready for the tackle). This is unusual as, at the top level, things happen very quickly and defenders have very little time to react.

When a ball carrier is strong and running at pace, a tackle made too high by a defender will get brushed off easily – the defender will be swatted away – and momentum is then conceded to the attackers. All things being equal, the player with more momentum in contact, be it attacker or defender, is more likely to get the result he wants.

Once brought to the ground, the tackled player must pass the ball immediately or place it on the ground and release it immediately. A tackled player must not intentionally push or place the ball in touch. However, if a player is merely knocked over and not still held by a tackler, they are not considered to have been tackled and they may get back up immediately and continue playing. If a tackle is made above the shoulder, or if a player does not make an attempt to wrap his arms around the player in the tackle (i.e. shoulder charging), the tackler will be penalised and may face a spell in the sin bin.

A tackler must release a tackled player immediately. He is obliged to make the ball available by making a proper attempt to roll away from the tackled player and the ball. The tackler is effectively out of the play until he gets back onto his feet – he cannot touch the ball, tackle another player or do anything, until he is back on his two feet. Once he is back on his feet, he can play the ball like any other player but does not have to come through the 'gate' like other players arriving to compete for the ball. This law also applies to the ball carrier. The next player to play the ball – be it a kick, pass or pick-and go himself – must be on his feet.

The Defensive System

The second element to a defence is organisation, where defenders work in prearranged systems that have been practised and perfected in training. Players defend as individuals (making the tackle) but there is a maxim in rugby that an isolated defender is a weak defender – as an isolated defender is easier to overcome and get past. Therefore, teams employ what is known as a 'defensive system' which is devised so that defenders are supported and assisted. A defence is only as strong as the weakest link in its chain.

The main purpose of a defensive system is to contain the opposition's attack. A defensive system will incorporate the approach to be taken by a defending team when the opposition has the ball at lineouts, scrums, kick restarts, at the breakdown and open-field play and is designed to cater for every area of the game – set piece or open play. Every defender knows where he should be, who he should be tackling and how to approach the tackle in any given situation when the opposition has possession. No defender is left unassisted or isolated, and therefore the defence is harder to overcome.

Today, defences are so organised that they drastically reduce the space available to attackers. Indeed, it now seems that defence is used as a form of attack, the idea being to put the opposition under sustained pressure and make them anxious about their attacks and therefore less ambitious. Tackle them before they reach the gainline and the attacking forwards must run back to help the tackled player and the momentum at the ruck shifts in the defence's favour – it is now easier to counter-ruck and cause a turnover or, at the very least, slow the opposition's ball and initiative.

It takes organisation, attitude and commitment by the defenders for defensive systems to work properly.

Basic Defensive Line Principles

There are several basic principles for a defence to master to prevent a successful attack.

◎ **Defend from the inside pushing out:** The defender starts inside his opponent (i.e. closer to the scrum/lineout/breakdown) forcing the attacker to drift wide and run out of space or limit the space for outside runners – the touchline is the defender's friend.

◎ **Come up together in a line:** Defensive lines will always come up together in a straight line (with the exception of the hook defence explained below) so that there are no dog-legs or fractures in the defensive line showing space that the opposition can take advantage of.

◎ **Reduce the attacking team's space:** Defensive lines will come forward aggressively to limit the space in which the opposition can attack. Space equals opportunities to break through the defence, as far as the attack is concerned.

Defensive Patterns

There are various defensive approaches which can be adopted by defenders when the opposition has possession.

◎ **Man-on-man defence:** The first and most basic pattern is the man-on-man defence. This is where defenders line up directly opposite their opposing player and push up in a line.

◎ **Drift defence:** This defence is generally employed at set pieces where the defending team's open-side flanker will cover the opposition fly-half leaving his own fly-half to defend the opposition first centre. This approach continues right across the defending backline with each defender marking the player outside his opposite number. All the defenders 'drift' across the pitch pushing the opposition towards the touchline and out of space.

◎ **Inside-pushing-out defence:** This involves the defenders moving up in a line, slightly inside their opposite numbers (i.e. closer to the scrum/lineout/breakdown), with the outside players in the defensive line staying slightly behind their team-mates on the inside, and all looking to push the attackers towards the sideline and out of space. The defenders start with the man-on-man approach but as soon as the defender's opposite number has passed the ball, the defender will drift onto the next opposing player signalling the entire defensive line to do likewise.

- ◎ **Outside-in/Hook defence:** This is the opposite of the inside-pushing-out defence. Here, the players on the outside of the defensive line rush up ahead of their team-mates on the inside and look to prevent the opposition fly-half passing the ball wide by blocking the path of his pass. Instead, they force him to play the ball closer to the defending pack where there are greater defending numbers.

- ◎ **Blitz/Rush defence:** This is where the defence sprints up in a line on the opposition hoping to take attacking space away from the attackers and make them panic into making a mistake, or be tackled as soon as they receive the ball, thus stopping the attack behind the gainline. More and more, this is becoming the most popular form of defence employed by the top teams. It puts attacking teams under massive pressure and, when successful, causes the attackers to be caught behind the gainline, so momentum changes over to the defending team. However, it is also a very risky defence because a defender travelling at full speed is easier to side-step as it is difficult for a defender to turn to tackle when he is running at full throttle.

- ◎ **Scramble defence:** This is a term given to describe the secondary defence employed by a team when their first line of defence has been breached by the attackers. The defenders chase back in numbers, make the tackle and hastily reorganise themselves to ensure there are no new gaps for the attackers to break through. This is when the game really opens up and the defence is put under maximum pressure. A defence will look to slow down the opposition ball by preventing the attacker from off-loading to a support runner or by legally contesting for the ball at the breakdown. Slowing down the ball enables the defence vital seconds to reorganise itself to ensure that the attackers are man marked and that no gaps appear for the attackers to target. It also causes attackers to mis-time their run and take the edge off the attack.

A well-drilled team will employ two or three different defensive patterns during a game depending on the situation they are faced with.

- From lineouts, a defending backline is most likely to use a drift defence because they are 20 metres away from the attacking backline and can see in good time what the attacking team is doing, or, the defending back row has not been engaged at the lineout and is free to join the backline in defence, swelling the defensive numbers, and enabling the other players to spread and cut down the space out wide.

- Generally at scrums, teams will rush forward and look to defend using the man-on-man defence first before changing to a drift defence if the attacking fly-half passes early.

- At the breakdown, defenders will start with 'pillars' standing on the side of the ruck/maul, but which are not part of the ruck/maul, who are responsible for defending against the first man in the attacking line (normally the scrum-half) – the rest of the defenders take their line off the pillar and will use one of the approaches mentioned earlier, depending on where the attackers have superior numbers – if its close to the ruck or maul, it will be a man-on-man or inside-pushing-out defence, if it is out wide, it will be a drift or hook defence.

- When close to the opposition's line, the defensive approach will alter slightly. The defence has fifteen defenders at its disposal, all in a line, as the defending wingers and full-back are now in line with the rest of the defenders. The defenders' concentration is at its optimum because they know just one small error on their part, be it an individual or collective error, will very easily result in a try for their opponents. The defenders will look to rush up quickly and desperately drive the attackers backwards in the tackle, away from the tryline.

Successful defending requires trust in one's team-mates, patience and discipline. Trust that one's team-mates will make their tackles so that a player can concentrate on his job and the opponent in front of him. Patience that the defence will hold out and, no matter how many phases of attack are hurled against it, it will not break. Discipline that a defender will not infringe and give away an easy 3-point, penalty-scoring chance.

7 INFRINGEMENTS

Penalties

There are approximately 600 possible infringements in a game of rugby. Indeed at scrum-time alone, there are seventy possible infringements that a referee must look out for. Some infringements deserve nothing more than a scrum being awarded against the offending team, some warrant a free kick, but most infringements cause the referee to award a penalty kick against the perpetrators. For penalty kicks and free kicks, the offending team must retire 10 metres and wait for the other team to take the penalty or free kick, as explained below, before they can move forward to defend.

Penalty Kicks

Penalty kicks can be taken as follows.

◎ A quick tap of the ball with the boot back into the penalty taker's hands before he runs with the ball. Normally done when the offending team is in the process of retiring 10 metres and cannot tackle the penalty taker until he has run at least 10 metres in any direction from the point of the infringement. A tap penalty is usually done when a team wishes to speed up the pace of a game and take advantage of the fact that the offending team's defence has not had time to align properly and, therefore, will have gaps in it that can be exploited. If the player taking the quick tap penalty is tackled before he has run 10 metres, the referee may stop play and punish the defence by awarding that player's side a further 10 metres. In which case, the attacking team must wait for the defence to retire 10 metres before taking the penalty. This quick tap penalty is often used by an attacking team near the halfway line in the hope that the extra 10 metres awarded will bring the attacking team within penalty kicking range (see the final point below).

- The ball is kicked straight to touch. The penalty takers get the throw-in into the lineout and therefore benefit from gaining territory from the kick and hopefully possession back from the lineout.

- If a penalty is awarded within kicking distance of the goalposts, a team may elect to have the kicker take an uncontested place kick at goal for 3 points from the spot on the pitch the referee determines the offence took place. If the kick is successful, 3 points are awarded and play is restarted at the halfway line with the non-scoring team kicking a drop-kick back to the scoring team. After an unsuccessful penalty kick, where the ball is kicked wide of the posts and over the dead-ball line or a defender catches it and touches it down, play is usually restarted with a 22-metre drop-out and is taken by the defending team.

Free Kicks

A free kick is just like a penalty kick except that it cannot be taken directly at goal and if it is kicked to touch, the other team is awarded the thrown-in at the lineout. If the free kick is taken outside that team's 22-metre zone, the ball must bounce before it goes into touch, just like a normal kick, otherwise the lineout will be taken back up the field opposite the point where the ball was kicked.

Ten Common Penalties Awarded Against a Team

Listed below are ten of the most common infringements that result in penalty kicks.

1. In defence, and before the ball leaves a scrum/maul/ruck, being in front of the hindmost foot of the player at the back of the scrum/maul/ruck when not involved in the scrum/ruck/maul.

2. Coming in from the side and not through the 'gate' at the tackle area.

3. Coming in from the side and not joining a ruck/maul from the back of the ruck/maul.

4. High tackle (a tackle above the shoulder).

5. Collapsing a maul.

6. Interfering with another player who does not have the ball (obstruction).

7. Not immediately releasing the ball after a tackle/in a ruck.

8. The tackler not immediately rolling away after he makes the tackle.

9. The defending back row not staying bound in a scrum before the attacking scrum-half or number 8 have their hands on the ball.

10. A player ahead of the kicker doesn't let the kicker, or one of his team-mates who started behind the kicker, run ahead of him and put him onside.

The Sin Bin

For persistent infringements, otherwise known as cynical penalties or professional fouls (where a defender intentionally gives away a penalty in the hope that play will be stopped and a try-scoring chance ruined), a referee will award a yellow card which means the offending player is temporarily dismissed from the game for ten minutes during which he must remain in the sin bin area on the sideline.

There is a fourth official who is responsible for timing the ten minutes, which are ten minutes of playing time and not actual time. So, if the referee stops the watch in order to speak to a player or touch judge about an incident, the ten-minute sin-bin countdown will also be stopped and not restarted until play resumes.

If a front-row player has been sin binned and has left the field of play to sit out his time, then at the next scrum during those ten minutes, the offending team must bring on a replacement front-row player and take off some other non-front-row player until the ten minutes has elapsed.

Two yellow cards result in permanent dismissal from the game. For the more serious offences, including punching another player or other forms of dangerous play, a player may receive a red card and be sent off.

Materiality

Sometimes, a referee may elect to ignore an offence, usually something minor, if he thinks it has not had a material effect on the game. Usually, the referee will have a quiet word with the offending player and warn him against recommitting the offence. This is done in order to let the game flow. Neither the players nor spectators wish play to be frustratingly halted every few seconds by the referee's whistle as he awards another penalty. Referees understand this and are willing to overlook minor indiscretions for the sake of allowing a game to open up.

Advantage

Very often an infringement will occur (e.g. knock-on, penalty, etc.) and the referee will allow the non-offending team to play on and take 'advantage' of the mistake in play. This is known as the Law of Advantage. The purpose of this law is to allow play be more continuous with fewer stoppages for infringements. Players are encouraged to play to the whistle despite infringements by the opposition. This period of playing the advantage is known as the 'window of opportunity'. The referee may allow play continue for a few seconds or for a few phases of play. The length of the window of opportunity is at the complete discretion of the referee and always the cause for much controversy. If no real gain occurs to the non-offending team in what the referee believes to be a reasonable period of time, he will whistle for play to be stopped and brought back to the place of the original infringement where he will award a scrum or penalty, as applicable. However, if after allowing advantage be played, the referee determines that the non-offending team has gained sufficiently he will say 'advantage over' and play continues as normal.

And Finally

Rugby has come a very long way since the days of William Webb Ellis. The game of rugby union today is a culmination of human skill, physical prowess and intelligent endeavour. It is faster, more exciting and physically demanding at a level never witnessed before. There have been dramatic changes in the laws of the game and the physique of the players themselves. These laws have been modified to meet the public's appetite for a thrilling spectacle of high speed physicality and, as a result, the game has been developed to keep the ball in play longer. Teams are constantly adapting their style of play to extract the maximum advantage from these law changes, which in turn has made the spectator's task of following the game that bit harder and yet so much more enjoyable!

8 GLOSSARY OF RUGBY TERMS

Term	Definition
advantage	When the referee allows play to continue after a team has infringed and the non-offending team has gained a better position.
against the head	A ball won by a team at a scrum when the opposition had the put-in.
binding	Holding on to a team-mate with the full use of an arm.
blind-side	The area between the ball and the nearest touchline. It is the narrow side of the pitch at a set piece or breakdown.
breakdown	The occasion during play, usually after a player has been tackled, when the ball is contested for by both teams.
charge down	A blocked kick.
chip kick	A short kick over the head of an on-rushing defender.
clearance kick	A kick down the pitch which relieves pressure.
conversion	A kick (either a place kick or drop-kick) taken after a try has been scored. If successful, a conversion is worth 2 points. The kick must be taken from a place opposite where the try was scored.
counter-attack	A counter-attack takes place immediately after the defending team has regained possession. Often the opportunity to counter attack occurs when the ball has been deliberately kicked by an opponent directly to the defending team.
crossing	Blocking an opponent in order to stop him tackling a team-mate by moving in front of the team-mate in order to act as a shield.
drop-kick	A kick employed when the kicker drops the ball to the ground and as it bounces back up he immediately kicks it.

drop-out	A drop-kick used to restart play after: (a) a missed penalty kick or drop goal attempt has passed the dead-ball line, or the ball has been touched down in the in-goal area by a defending player; or (b) the attacking team has kicked the ball into (or lost control of the ball) the in-goal area and the defending team touches down the ball. The ball is drop kicked back to the original attacking team from anywhere behind the defending team's 22-metre line.
dummy pass	A fake pass.
fair catch	A catch by a player from behind his 22-metre line where he calls 'mark' as he catches the ball. The referee will award a free kick to the catcher from the spot he caught the ball. The player's feet may be in the air or on the ground when he catches the ball.
feed	Also known as the 'put-in'. It is the act of rolling the ball into the scrum by the scrum-half.
field of play	The area of the pitch between the trylines and the touchlines. These lines are not part of the field of play.
forward pass	An illegal pass to a player who is ahead of the ball.
free kick	Awarded by a referee following certain infringements. It cannot be taken directly at goal and if it is kicked to touch, the other team is awarded the throw-in at the lineout.
gainline	An imaginary line across the pitch that signifies the mid-point between the attacking team and the defending team. When crossed, it signifies territorial advantage to the team that has crossed the line.
gate	The entry zone into a tackle area through which supporting players must enter to avoid being penalised.
grounding the ball	The act of holding the ball and touching the ground with it or pressing down on the ball on the ground with a player's hands, arms or the front of his body from waist to neck inclusive, in the opposition's in-goal area when scoring a try.
grubber kick	A kick along the ground.
hit	In a scrum, it describes the engagement when both packs collide and interlock. In a tackle, it is the act of making contact with the tackler's shoulder.

IRB	International Rugby Board. The world governing and law-making body for the game of rugby union.
IRFU	Irish Rugby Football Union
injury time	Extra time added to the end of a half to compensate for time stoppage due to injuries.
into contact	The act of taking the ball into a tackle situation.
in-goal	The area of the pitch between the tryline and the dead-ball line, and between the touch-in-goal lines. A try can be scored either on or over the tryline once it is within the in-goal area.
knock on	When the ball hits off a player's arm or hand and drops forward.
lineout	A method employed to restart play after the ball goes into touch. The ball is thrown down the middle of two single-file lines formed by each team.
mark	A spot or place on the pitch. Also, the word called out by a player taking a fair catch behind his 22-metre line.
maul	A loose formation around the ball carrier when he has been held up off the ground and which involves both teams wrestling for possession.
obstruction	Standing in front of an opponent preventing him from playing the ball.
offside	Standing in an illegal position on the pitch. Usually occurs when a player is in front of the ball after it was last played by a team-mate.
open-side	The area between the ball and the furthest touchline, and which has the most space in which to launch an attack.
overlap	When a team has more players in attack than the other team has in defence.
out wide	The place on the pitch furthest from the scrum/lineout/breakdown.
peel/peeling	When a forward is fed the ball by the jumper in the lineout and the forward then runs around the side of the lineout.

penalty kick	A kick awarded to the non-offending team after a law has been broken and for which a penalty kick is the applicable punishment. The ball can be kicked straight to touch and the kicking team will have the throw-in or it can be aimed at the goalposts if in kicking distance. If it goes between the posts and over the crossbar, it is worth 3 points.
penalty try	Awarded when the referee deems a try would almost certainly have been scored but for an infringement by the opposition.
place kick	A kick technique where the ball is placed and tee'd up on the ground before being kicked.
phase of play	A segment in play between when the ball is taken into contact by an attacking player and recycled, and the next breakdown. Kick-off or set pieces are described as the first phase of play.
ruck	A loose formation involving both teams trying to push each other off the ball, which is on the ground in open play.
scrum	Another method used to restart play. It involves both sets of forwards in tight formation trying to push each other off the ball which has been fed into the tunnel in the middle by the attacking scrum-half.
scrummaging	The process of setting and completing a scrum.
set piece	A means of restarting play by way of a scrum or lineout.
sin bin	A seat on the sideline where a player must stay for ten minutes of actual play in order to serve out a temporary suspension for a professional or cynical foul including persistent infringement.
Six Nations Championship	Annual tournament of international rugby held in northern hemisphere between England, France, Ireland, Wales, Scotland and Italy.
Super 14	Southern hemisphere competition made up of the top fourteen provincial teams from New Zealand (five teams), Australia (four teams) and South Africa (five teams).
tap down	When the jumper deflects the throw-in in a lineout towards the scrum-half or to a forward peeling around.

tap penalty	Used when a team wishes to take a penalty quickly and run with the ball. The player taking the penalty drops the ball out of his hands and 'taps' the ball lightly with his boot before reclaiming the ball.
throw in	Throwing the ball down the middle of a lineout.
touch	When the ball touches the touchline or the ground beyond it and is therefore out of play.
touchline	Also known as the sideline. A boundary line on either side of the pitch. When the ball touches this line or the ground beyond this line, or is carried by a player over this line, it is no longer in play and must be put back in play by means of a lineout.
try	Method of scoring, worth 5 points, by touching down the ball on or over the tryline in the opponents' in-goal area.
turnover	The conceding of possession from one team to the other during play. Usually used to describe the act of winning the ball back from the opposition at the breakdown.
up-and-under	A high kick that does not travel far down the pitch and which is intended to stay in the field of play. Also known as a Garryowen.